The .... *to*

CRITICAL THINKING

Concepts and Tools

EIGHTH EDITION

RICHARD PAUL and LINDA ELDER

ROWMAN & LITTLEFIELD
Lanham • Boulder • New York • London

Published by Rowman & Littlefield
An imprint of The Rowman & Littlefield Publishing Group, Inc.
4501 Forbes Boulevard, Suite 200, Lanham, Maryland 20706
www.rowman.com

6 Tinworth Street, London SE11 5AL, United Kingdom

British Library Cataloguing in Publication Information Available

Library of Congress Cataloging-in-Publication Data available

ISBN 9781538134948 (pbk. : alk. paper)
ISBN 9781538134955 (electronic)

∞™ The paper used in this publication meets the minimum requirements of
American National Standard for Information Sciences—Permanence of Paper for
Printed Library Materials, ANSI/NISO Z39.48-1992.

The Foundation for Critical Thinking and the Thinker's Guide Library

Founded by Dr. Richard Paul, the Foundation for Critical Thinking is the longest-running non-profit organization dedicated to critical thinking. Through seminars and conferences, online courses and resources, and a wide range of publications, the Foundation promotes critical societies through cultivating essential intellectual abilities and virtues across every field of study and professional area. Visit them at www.criticalthinking.org and learn about the Center for Critical Thinking Community Online.

The Thinker's Guide Library presents the framework of critical thinking across subject areas and audience levels to foster integration of critical reasoning throughout our world.

1. The Miniature Guide to Critical Thinking Concepts and Tools, Eighth Edition
2. The Thinker's Guide to Analytic Thinking
3. The Aspiring Thinker's Guide to Critical Thinking
4. The Thinker's Guide to Ethical Reasoning
5. The Thinker's Guide to Socratic Questioning
6. The Thinker's Guide to Fallacies
7. The Art of Asking Essential Questions, Fifth Edition
8. Student Guide to Historical Thinking
9. Thinker's Guide to the Human Mind
10. The Thinker's Guide to Scientific Thinking
11. The Thinker's Guide to Clinical Reasoning
12. The Thinker's Guide to Engineering Reasoning
13. The Nature and Functions of Critical & Creative Thinking
14. The Thinker's Guide for Conscientious Citizens on How to Detect Media Bias and Propaganda in National and World News, Fourth Edition
15. The Thinker's Guide for Students on How to Study & Learn a Discipline, Second Edition
16. How to Read a Paragraph: The Art of Close Reading, Second Edition
17. How to Write a Paragraph: The Art of Substantive Writing
18. The International Critical Thinking Reading and Writing Test, Second Edition
19. The Thinker's Guide to Intellectual Standards
20. A Critical Thinker's Guide to Educational Fads
21. The Miniature Guide to Practical Ways for Promoting Active and Cooperative Learning, Third Edition
22. How to Improve Student Learning: 30 Practical Ideas
23. A Guide for Educators to Critical Thinking Competency Standards

Rowman & Littlefield is the proud distributor of the Thinker's Guide Library. Please visit www.rowman.com or call 1-800-462-640 for more information.

Dedication to Richard Paul

This book is dedicated to the life and work of Richard W. Paul (1937–2015), one of the few truly original thinkers and scholars in the field of critical thinking studies, who dedicated his life to understanding and illuminating the essential, the most foundational, and the most integrated core concepts and principles in critical thinking. Through these intellectual tools and, further, by insisting upon strong sense or fairminded critical thinking, Paul revolutionized the theory and course of critical thinking.

About the Authors

 Dr. Linda Elder is an educational psychologist who has taught both psychology and critical thinking at the college level. She is the president of the Foundation for Critical Thinking and executive director of the Center for Critical Thinking. Dr. Elder has a special interest in the relation of thought and emotion, the cognitive and the affective, and has developed an original theory of the stages of critical thinking development. She has coauthored four books on critical thinking, as well as twenty-five Thinker's Guides. She is a dynamic presenter with extensive experience in leading workshops on critical thinking.

 Dr. Richard Paul was a leading proponent of critical thinking until his death in August of 2015. In his work and legacy, Paul remains an international authority on critical thinking. He founded the Center for Critical Thinking at Sonoma State University in 1980, followed by the Foundation for Critical Thinking. In his lifetime, he developed concepts, principles, and theory essential to a robust and fairminded conception of critical thinking; he worked tenaciously to advance ethical, or strong-sense, critical thinking throughout education and society. In his lifetime, Paul authored more than two hundred articles and seven books on critical thinking. He presented workshops to hundreds of thousands of educators over his thirty-five-year history as a primary leader in the critical thinking movement.

Contents

The Human Minds Is Frequently Irrational While Having the Capacity for Rational Thought

Introduction

This small but powerful book contains core critical thinking concepts and principles distilled into compact size. These principles are universally applicable to human reasoning in every legitimate academic field, discipline, and profession. They give rise to the skills, abilities, and characteristics of those who think critically; they illuminate innate barriers to criticality.

Throughout human history, the concept of critical thinking has been treated, on the whole, superficially. Within academic disciplines, critical reasoning is still largely misunderstood or ignored. Yet the only way to understand any subject is to reason through problems and issues within that subject using one's own reasoning. When you develop skill in reasoning your way through questions within an academic discipline and begin formulating questions of your own, you are learning to think like a scholar.

Critical thinkers routinely clarify their purposes and the questions at issue in a given situation or context. They question information, conclusions, and points of view. They strive to be clear, accurate, precise, and relevant. They do not distort information or use false information in arguing for their position. They act in good faith in relation to others and in representing others' views. They look beneath the surface; they are logical and reasonable. They apply critical reasoning skills to their reading and writing, as well as to their speaking and listening. They apply these skills in history, science, math, philosophy, the arts, and professional and personal life.

Developing as a critical thinker entails explicitly focusing on the naturally occurring processes in your reasoning and learning to intervene in your poor-quality reasoning. It means developing a keen interest in how your mind moves cognitively from one idea to another, in what causes these particular moves to occur rather than others, and in how to intervene in the process when flaws are uncovered in any of your thinking. Put another way, critical thinkers have an abiding interest in the problematic aspects of their own thinking, and they seek out these problem areas, target them, and change something about their thinking in order to reason more rationally, logically, and justifiably. Embracing critical thinking means learning to take command of the thoughts that control you, thereby experiencing a happier, more satisfied inner sense of self.

This newest edition of *The Miniature Guide to Critical Thinking Concepts and Tools* contains all the original work from our previous version and continues to unpack and contextualize the theoretical work found in the original guide—focusing fundamentally on the elements of reasoning, universal intellectual standards, and intellectual virtues or character traits. This book offers additional critical thinking theory and strategies for improving reasoning within the various parts of human life and human study, which will help readers better internalize the basic tools of critical thinking and apply them within subjects and fields. More material has been included in this book on the barriers to critical thinking to help the reader come to terms with the power of these barriers to impede critical thought. We place these impediments under the broad categories of egocentric and sociocentric thought, which account for such common phenomena as closemindedness, self-deception, rationalization, intellectual arrogance, hypocrisy, greed, selfishness, herd mentality, prejudice, and many other pathological ways in which people think, feel, and act. Finally, we end with an elaboration on our conception of critical societies and what would be widely or universally valued in human life, were critical thinking ever to become a far-reaching reality.

This book opens up many avenues for improving personal and professional decisions through critical thinking. For students, it is a critical thinking supplement to any textbook for any course, as it lays foundations for reasoning through all subjects, disciplines, and professions. For faculty, it provides a shared concept of critical thinking. Faculty can use this book to design instruction, assignments, and assessment methods in any subject. When this guide is used as a supplement to the textbook in multiple courses, students begin to perceive the usefulness of critical thinking in every domain of learning. If their instructors provide examples of the application of the subject to daily life, students begin to properly perceive education as a tool for improving the quality of their lives.

If you are a student using this guide, consult it frequently in analyzing and synthesizing what you are learning. Aim for deep internalization of the principles you find in it—until using them becomes second nature. If successful, this guide will serve faculty, students, and the public simultaneously.

Why Critical Thinking?

The Problem:

Everyone thinks; it is our nature to do so. But much of our thinking, left to itself, is biased, distorted, partial, uninformed, or downright prejudiced. Yet the quality of our life and that of what we produce, make, or build depends precisely on the quality of our thought. Shoddy thinking is costly, both in money and in quality of life. Excellence in thought, however, must be systematically cultivated.

A Definition:

Critical thinking is the art of analyzing and evaluating thought processes with a view to improving them. Critical thinking is self-directed, self-disciplined, self-monitored, and self-corrective thinking. It requires rigorous standards of excellence and mindful command of their use. It entails effective communication and problem solving abilities, as well as a commitment to overcoming our native egocentrism and sociocentrism. It advances the character and ethical sensitivities of the dedicated person through the explicit cultivation of intellectual virtues.

The Result:

A well-cultivated critical thinker:

• raises vital questions and problems, formulating them clearly and precisely;
• gathers and assesses relevant information, using abstract ideas to interpret it effectively;
• comes to well-reasoned conclusions and solutions, testing them against relevant criteria and standards;
• thinks openmindedly within alternative systems of thought, recognizing and assessing, as need be, their assumptions, implications, and practical consequences;
• communicates effectively with others in figuring out solutions to complex problems; and
• is scrupulously careful not to misrepresent or distort information in developing an argument or position, and sees through false information and fake news.

Stages of Critical Thinking Development

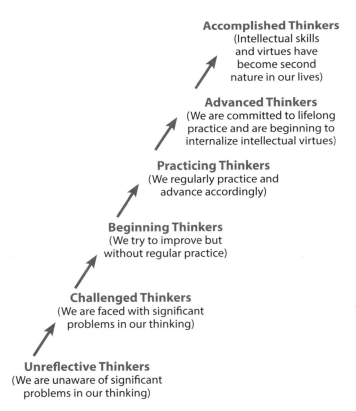

Accomplished Thinkers
(Intellectual skills
and virtues have
become second
nature in our lives)

Advanced Thinkers
(We are committed to lifelong
practice and are beginning to
internalize intellectual virtues)

Practicing Thinkers
(We regularly practice and
advance accordingly)

Beginning Thinkers
(We try to improve but
without regular practice)

Challenged Thinkers
(We are faced with significant
problems in our thinking)

Unreflective Thinkers
(We are unaware of significant
problems in our thinking)

A Substantive Approach to Critical Thinking

A useful concept of critical thinking includes the disciplined analysis and assessment of reasoning as one cultivates intellectual virtues. This process entails concern for two primary barriers to criticality—egocentric and sociocentric thinking—which are prevalent and widespread in human thought and life.

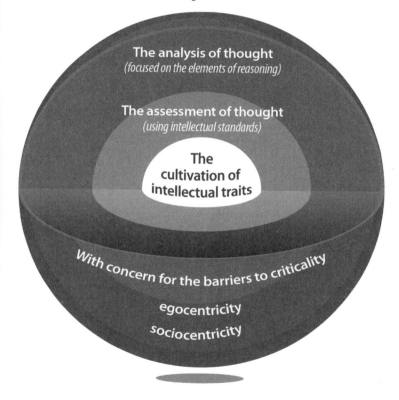

The analysis of thought
(focused on the elements of reasoning)

The assessment of thought
(using intellectual standards)

The cultivation of intellectual traits

With concern for the barriers to criticality

egocentricity

sociocentricity

Critical Thinkers Routinely Apply Intellectual Standards to the Elements of Reasoning

Those who adhere to relevant intellectual standards when reasoning through issues in the essential parts of human life develop intellectual virtues increasingly over time.

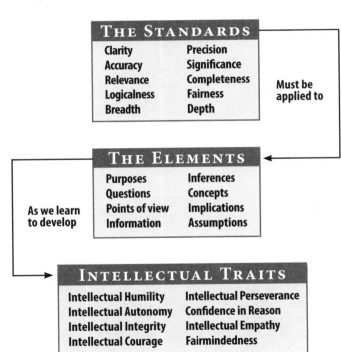

THE STANDARDS

Clarity	Precision
Accuracy	Significance
Relevance	Completeness
Logicalness	Fairness
Breadth	Depth

Must be applied to

THE ELEMENTS

Purposes	Inferences
Questions	Concepts
Points of view	Implications
Information	Assumptions

As we learn to develop

INTELLECTUAL TRAITS

Intellectual Humility	Intellectual Perseverance
Intellectual Autonomy	Confidence in Reason
Intellectual Integrity	Intellectual Empathy
Intellectual Courage	Fairmindedness

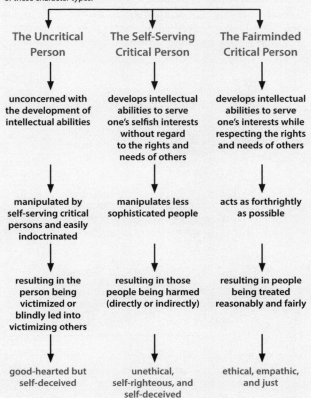

Three Types of Character

The Fairminded Critical Person aspires to embody intellectual virtues in all situations. The Self-Serving Critical Person is skilled at reasoning but generally not concerned with the rights of others. The Uncritical Person is unconcerned with thought and therefore easily manipulated. In reality, every person embodies some part of each of these character types.

The Uncritical Person	The Self-Serving Critical Person	The Fairminded Critical Person
unconcerned with the development of intellectual abilities	develops intellectual abilities to serve one's selfish interests without regard to the rights and needs of others	develops intellectual abilities to serve one's interests while respecting the rights and needs of others
manipulated by self-serving critical persons and easily indoctrinated	manipulates less sophisticated people	acts as forthrightly as possible
resulting in the person being victimized or blindly led into victimizing others	resulting in those people being harmed (directly or indirectly)	resulting in people being treated reasonably and fairly
good-hearted but self-deceived	unethical, self-righteous, and self-deceived	ethical, empathic, and just

The Elements of Thought

Eight Elements Define All Reasoning

Eight basic structures are present in all thinking: Whenever we think, we think for a purpose within a point of view based on assumptions that lead to implications and consequences. We use concepts, ideas, and theories to interpret data, facts, and experiences in order to answer questions, solve problems, and resolve issues.

Thinking, then:

- generates purposes

- raises questions

- uses information

- utilizes concepts

- makes inferences

- makes assumptions

- generates implications

- embodies a point of view

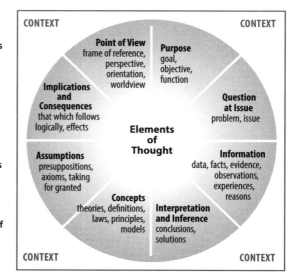

Critical thinkers use the elements of reasoning with sensitivity to universal intellectual criteria, or standards, such as clarity, precision, accuracy, relevance, significance, depth, breadth, logicalness, sufficiency, and fairness.

Questions Using the Elements of Thought

Remember that the elements of reasoning are embedded in all reasoning, both your own and that of others. Use these questions to open up and deconstruct reasoning when writing a paper or reading something for class or of significance to you personally.

Purpose: **What am I trying to accomplish?**
                        What is my central aim? My purpose?

Questions: **What question am I raising?**
                        What questions should we be addressing?
                        Am I considering the complexities in the question?

Information: **What information am I using in coming to this conclusion?**
                        What information do I need to settle the question?
                        How do I know the information is true?

Inferences/   **How did I reach this conclusion?**
Conclusions: **Is there another way to interpret the information?**

Concepts: **What is the main idea here?**
                        Can I explain this idea?

Assumptions: **What am I taking for granted?**
                        What assumption has led me to this conclusion?

Implications/   **If someone accepted my position, what would be some of**
Consequences: **the important implications? In other words, what might**
                        follow?
                        What am I implying?

Points of View: **From what point of view am I looking at this issue?**
                        Is there another point of view I should consider?

© 2020 Linda Elder   *www.criticalthinking.org*

A Checklist for Reasoning

1) All reasoning has a PURPOSE.

- Can you state your purpose clearly?
- What is the objective of your reasoning?
- Does your reasoning stay focused throughout on your goal?
- Is your purpose fair in context, considering all relevant persons or other species?
- Is your goal realistic?

2) All reasoning is an attempt to figure something out, to settle some QUESTION, or to solve some PROBLEM.

- What main question are you trying to answer?
- Are there other ways to think about the question?
- Can you divide the question into sub-questions?
- What questions would you need to ask and answer before you could answer the main question?
- Is this a question that has one right answer or can there be more than one reasonable answer?
- Does this question require judgment rather than facts alone?

3) All reasoning is based on ASSUMPTIONS.

- What assumptions are you making? Are they justified?
- How are your assumptions shaping your point of view?
- Which of your assumptions might reasonably be questioned?

4) All reasoning is done from some POINT OF VIEW.

- What is your point of view? What insights is it based on? What are its weaknesses?
- What other points of view should be considered in reasoning through this problem? What are the strengths and weaknesses of these viewpoints? Are you fairmindedly considering the insights behind these viewpoints?

5) All reasoning is based on DATA, INFORMATION, and EVIDENCE.

- To what extent is your reasoning supported by relevant data?
- How can you make sure your reasoning is based on information that is accurate or true?
- How do you know you are not distorting information to fit your selfish or vested interests?
- Do the data suggest explanations that differ from those you have given?
- How clear, accurate, and relevant are the data to the question at issue?
- Have you gathered sufficient data to reach a reasonable conclusion?

6) All reasoning is expressed through, and shaped by, CONCEPTS and THEORIES.

- What key ideas and theories are guiding your reasoning?
- What alternative explanations might be possible, given these concepts and theories?
- Do you deliberately take command of the ideas that guide your reasoning and control the quality of your life?
- Are you distorting ideas to fit your agenda?

7) All reasoning contains INFERENCES or INTERPRETATIONS by which we draw CONCLUSIONS and give meaning to data.

- To what extent do the data support your conclusions?
- Are your inferences consistent with each other?
- Are there other reasonable inferences that should be considered?
- Are you able to consider alternative possibilities when coming to conclusions, or do you lock yourself into one way of interpreting situations?

8) All reasoning leads somewhere and has IMPLICATIONS and CONSEQUENCES.

- What implications and consequences follow from your reasoning?
- If we accept your line of reasoning, what implications or consequences are likely?
- If you decide to do X, what might immediately follow from your decision? What might follow from acting upon that decision in the long run as the implications and consequences spiral out?

The Figuring Mind

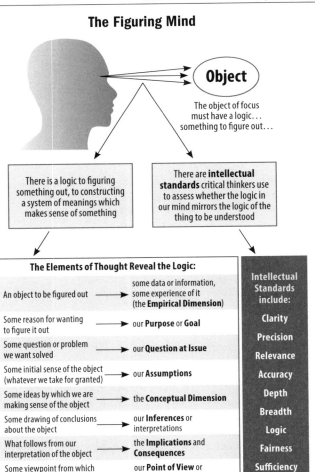

Object

The object of focus must have a logic... something to figure out...

There is a logic to figuring something out, to constructing a system of meanings which makes sense of something

There are **intellectual standards** critical thinkers use to assess whether the logic in our mind mirrors the logic of the thing to be understood

The Elements of Thought Reveal the Logic:

1	An object to be figured out	→ some data or information, some experience of it (the **Empirical Dimension**)
2	Some reason for wanting to figure it out	→ our **Purpose** or **Goal**
3	Some question or problem we want solved	→ our **Question at Issue**
4	Some initial sense of the object (whatever we take for granted)	→ our **Assumptions**
5	Some ideas by which we are making sense of the object	→ the **Conceptual Dimension**
6	Some drawing of conclusions about the object	→ our **Inferences** or interpretations
7	What follows from our interpretation of the object	→ the **Implications** and **Consequences**
8	Some viewpoint from which we conceptualize the object	→ our **Point of View** or **Frame of Reference**

Intellectual Standards include:

Clarity

Precision

Relevance

Accuracy

Depth

Breadth

Logic

Fairness

Sufficiency

Universal Intellectual Standards

And Questions That Can Be Used to Apply Them

To be effective thinkers, we must go beyond taking thinking apart. We also must apply standards to the elements of reasoning to assess our thinking and ensure its quality. Routine, consistent, and deliberate application of intellectual standards to reasoning, over time, leads to the cultivation of intellectual virtues. To be learned, these standards must be taught explicitly. The ultimate goal is for these standards to become infused in your thinking, forming part of your inner voice and guiding you to reason better.

Clarity

Clarity is a gateway standard. If a statement is unclear, we cannot determine whether it is accurate or relevant. In fact, we cannot tell anything about it because we don't yet know what it is saying. For example, the question "What can be done about the education system in America?" is unclear. In order to adequately address the question, we would need to have a clearer understanding of what the person asking the question is considering the "problem" to be. A clearer question might be "What can educators do to ensure that students learn the skills and abilities which help them function successfully on the job and in their daily decision-making?"

Accuracy

A statement can be clear but not accurate, as in "Most dogs weigh more than 300 pounds."

Precision

A statement can be both clear and accurate but not precise, as in "Jack is overweight." (We don't know how overweight Jack is, one pound or 500 pounds.)

Relevance

A statement can be clear, accurate, and precise but not relevant to the question at issue. For example, students often think that the amount of effort they put into a course should be used in raising their grade in a course. Often, however, "effort" does not measure the quality of student learning, and when that is so, effort is irrelevant to their appropriate grade.

Depth

A statement can be clear, accurate, precise, and relevant, but superficial (that is, it lacks depth). For example, the slogan "Just Say No", which was used for a number of years to discourage children and teens from using drugs, is clear, accurate, precise, and relevant. Nevertheless, those who use this approach treat a highly complex issue—the pervasive problem of drug use among young people—superficially. It fails to deal with the complexities of the issue.

Breadth

A line of reasoning may be clear, accurate, precise, relevant, and deep but lack breadth (as in an argument from either conservative or liberal standpoints that gets deeply into an issue but only recognizes the insights of one side of the question).

Logic

When we think, we bring a variety of thoughts together into some order. When the combination of thoughts are mutually supporting and make sense in combination, the thinking is "logical." When the combination is not mutually supporting, is contradictory in some sense, or does not "make sense," the combination is "not logical."

Fairness

We naturally think from our own perspective, from a point of view that tends to privilege our position. Fairness implies the treating of all relevant viewpoints alike without reference to one's own feelings or interests. Because we tend to be biased in favor of our own viewpoint, it is important to keep the standard of fairness at the forefront of our thinking. This is especially important when the situation may call on us to see things we don't want to see or give something up that we want to hold onto.

Some Essential Intellectual Standards for All Human Thought

Clarity	Could you elaborate further? Could you give me an example? Could you illustrate what you mean?
Accuracy	How could we check on that? How could we find out if that is true? How could we verify or test that?
Precision	Could you be more specific? Could you give me more details? Could you be more exact?
Relevance	How does that relate to the problem? How does that bear on the question? How does that help us with the issue?
Depth	What factors make this a difficult problem? What are some of the complexities of this question? What are some of the difficulties we need to deal with?
Breadth	Do we need to look at this from another perspective? Do we need to consider another point of view? Do we need to look at this in other ways?
Logic	Does all this make sense together? Does your first paragraph fit in with your last? Does what you say follow from the evidence?
Significance	Is this the most important problem to consider? Is this the central idea to focus on? Which of these facts are most important?
Fairness	Do I have any vested interest in this issue? Am I sympathetically representing the viewpoints of others? Have we fully and fairly considered all the important information relevant to the issue?
Sufficiency	Do we have sufficient information to answer the question? Are we unfairly leaving out information we would rather not consider in order to get more for our group while ignoring or downplaying the rights and needs of others?

Where Do Intellectual Standards Come From?

Intellectual standards ultimately derive from the nature of thought itself and what we characteristically need thought to do.

- Thus, the intellectual standard of *clarity* derives from the fact that we want or need to communicate a certain meaning to others, and unclear language undermines or defeats that purpose.
- The intellectual standard of *accuracy* derives from the fact that we are trying to understand or communicate things as they actually are, without any distortions. Inaccurate thought defeats that purpose.
- The intellectual standard of *precision* derives from the fact that we often need details and specifics to accomplish our purpose. Imprecision, or the failure to provide details and specifics, defeats that purpose.
- The intellectual standard of *relevance* derives from the fact that some information—however true it might be—does not bear upon a question to which we need an answer. Irrelevant information, thrust into the thinking process, diverts us from the information we do need and prevents us from answering the question at hand.
- The intellectual standard of *depth* derives from the fact that some issues involve complexity, and thinking that ignores these complexities is necessarily inadequate.
- The intellectual standard of *breadth* derives from the fact that some issues can be dealt with only by reasoning within multiple points of view. Thinking that is one-sided when many-sidedness is called for cannot be adequate.
- The intellectual standard of *logic* derives from the fact that reasoning that is inconsistent and self-contradictory necessarily lacks intelligibility.
- The intellectual standard of *fairness* derives from the fact that humans commonly ignore relevant facts and insights when they are not in line with one's interest or agenda.
- The intellectual standard of *sufficiency* derives from the fact that it is possible to gather detailed and vast information that is relevant and accurate, but that is still not sufficient to answer the question at issue or solve the problem at hand.

To generalize, it would be unintelligible to say, "I want to reason well, but I am indifferent as to whether my reasoning is clear, precise, accurate, relevant, logical, consistent, or fair."

Intellectual Virtues of the
Fairminded Critical Thinker

Fairminded thinkers pursue their own needs, desires, and goals while also considering, to the same degree and in good faith, the rights and needs of others. Yet it is possible to learn to use one's skills of mind in a narrow, self-serving way—many highly skilled thinkers do just that. Those who wish to develop as ethical critical reasoners work to embody the following character traits:

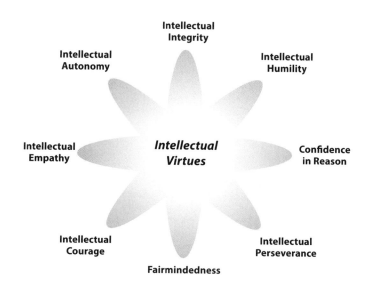

Intellectual
Integrity

Intellectual
Autonomy

Intellectual
Humility

Intellectual
Empathy

*Intellectual
Virtues*

Confidence
in Reason

Intellectual
Courage

Intellectual
Perseverance

Fairmindedness

Essential Intellectual Traits

Fairminded critical reasoners cultivate not only intellectual abilities but also intellectual dispositions. These attributes are essential to excellence of thought. They determine with what insight and integrity you think. Here we briefly describe the intellectual virtues and provide related questions that foster their development. Only to the extent that you routinely and abidingly ask these questions of yourself are you able to develop these virtues.

Intellectual Humility   vs   Intellectual Arrogance

Having a consciousness of the limits of one's knowledge, including a sensitivity to circumstances in which one's native egocentrism is likely to function self-deceptively, as well as a sensitivity to bias, prejudice, and the limitations of one's viewpoint. Intellectual humility depends on recognizing that one should not claim more than one actually knows. It does not imply spinelessness or submissiveness. It implies the lack of intellectual pretentiousness, boastfulness, or conceit, combined with insight into the logical foundations, or lack of such foundations, of one's beliefs.

- What do I really know (about myself, about the situation, about another person, about my nation, about what is going on in the world)?
- To what extent do my prejudices or biases influence my thinking?
- To what extent have I been indoctrinated into beliefs that may be false?
- How do the beliefs I have uncritically accepted keep me from seeing things as they are?

Intellectual Courage   vs   Intellectual Cowardice

Having a consciousness of the need to face and fairly address ideas, beliefs, or viewpoints toward which we have strong negative emotions and to which we have not given a serious hearing. This courage is connected with the recognition that ideas we consider dangerous or absurd are sometimes rationally justified (in whole or in part) and that conclusions and beliefs inculcated in us are sometimes false or misleading. To determine for ourselves which is which, we must not passively and uncritically accept what we have "learned." Intellectual courage comes into play here, because inevitably we will come to see some truth in some ideas considered dangerous and absurd, and distortion or falsity in some ideas strongly held in our social group. We need courage to be true to our own thinking in such circumstances. The penalties for nonconformity can be severe.

- To what extent have I analyzed the beliefs I hold?
- To what extent have I questioned my beliefs, many of which I learned in childhood?
- To what extent have I demonstrated a willingness to give up my beliefs when sufficient evidence is presented against them?
- To what extent am I willing to stand up against the majority, even though people might ridicule me?

Intellectual Empathy   vs   Intellectual Narrow-mindedness

Having a consciousness of the need to imaginatively put oneself in the place of others in order to genuinely understand them, which requires the consciousness of our egocentric tendency to identify truth with our immediate perceptions of long-standing thought or belief. This trait correlates with the ability to reconstruct accurately the viewpoints and reasoning of others and to reason from premises, assumptions, and ideas other than our own. This trait also correlates with the willingness to remember occasions when we were wrong in the past despite an intense conviction that we were right, and with the ability to imagine our being similarly deceived in the case at hand.

Intellectual Autonomy   vs   Intellectual Conformity

Having rational control of one's beliefs, values, and inferences. The ideal of critical thinking is to learn to think for oneself, to gain command over one's thought processes. It entails a commitment to analyzing and evaluating beliefs on the basis of reason and evidence, to question when it is rational to question, to believe when it is rational to believe, and to conform when it is rational to conform.

- To what extent am I a conformist?
- To what extent do I uncritically accept what I am told by my government, the media, or my peers?
- Do I think through issues on my own, or do I merely accept the views of others?
- Having thought through an issue from a rational perspective, am I willing to stand alone despite the irrational criticisms of others?

Intellectual Integrity   vs   Intellectual Hypocrisy

Recognition of the need to be true to one's own thinking; to be consistent in the intellectual standards one applies; to hold one's self to the same rigorous standards of evidence and proof to which one holds one's antagonists; to practice what one advocates for others; and to honestly admit discrepancies and inconsistencies in one's own thought and action.

- Do I behave in accordance with what I say I believe, or do I tend to say one thing and do another?
- To what extent do I expect the same of myself as I expect of others?
- To what extent are there contradictions or inconsistencies in my life?
- To what extent do I strive to recognize and eliminate self-deception in my life?

Intellectual Perseverance   vs   Intellectual Laziness

Having a consciousness of the need to use intellectual insights and truths in spite of difficulties, obstacles, and frustrations; firm adherence to rational principles despite the irrational opposition of others; a sense of the need to struggle with confusion and unsettled questions over an extended period of time to achieve deeper understanding or insight.

- Am I willing to work my way through complexities in an issue, or do I tend to give up when I experience difficulty?
- Can I think of a difficult intellectual problem in which I have demonstrated patience and determination in working through the difficulties?
- Do I have strategies for dealing with complex problems?
- Do I expect learning to be easy, or do I recognize the importance of engaging in challenging intellectual work?

Confidence in Reason   vs   Distrust of Reason and Evidence

Confidence that, in the long run, one's own higher interests and those of humankind at large will be best served by giving the freest play to reason and by encouraging people to come to their own conclusions by developing their own rational faculties; faith that, with proper encouragement and cultivation, people can learn to think for themselves, to form rational viewpoints, draw reasonable conclusions, think coherently and logically, persuade each other by reason, and become reasonable persons, despite the deep-seated obstacles in the native character of the human mind and in society as we know it.

- Am I willing to change my position when the evidence leads to a more reasonable position?
- Do I adhere to principles of sound reasoning when persuading others of my position, or do I distort matters to support my position?
- Do I deem it more important to "win" an argument or to see the issue from the most reasonable perspective?
- Do I encourage others to come to their own conclusions, or do I try to force my views on them?

Fairmindedness   vs   Intellectual Unfairness

Having a consciousness of the need to treat all viewpoints alike, without reference to one's own feelings or vested interests, or the feelings or vested interests of one's friends, community, or nation; implies adherence to intellectual standards without reference to one's own advantage or the advantage of one's group.

- To what extent do self-interests or biases tend to cloud my judgment?
- How do I tend to treat relevant viewpoints? Do I tend to favor some over others? If so, why?
- To what extent do I appropriately weigh the strengths and weaknesses of all significant relevant perspectives when reasoning through an issue?
- What personal interests do we have at stake here and how can we ensure that we don't favor our own interests over the common good?

How Intellectual Virtues Are Interrelated

The characteristics of mind essential to fairminded critical thinking are interdependent. Each requires the others to advance reasoning to the highest levels of skill and justifiability. Consider *intellectual humility*: To become aware of the limits of your knowledge, you need the *intellectual courage* to face your prejudices and ignorance. To discover your own prejudices, in turn, you often must *intellectually empathize* with and *fairmindedly* reason within viewpoints with which you disagree. Achieving this end typically requires *intellectual perseverance* because learning to enter viewpoints that differ from your own can take significant effort, requiring you to work your way through misconceptions, uncover faulty assumptions you have been using in your thinking, and rework these assumptions to fit a more reasonable or logical picture of reality. This effort will not seem reasonable unless you have the necessary *confidence in reason* to believe you will not be tainted or "taken in" by false or misleading ideas in considering alternative views.

Furthermore, merely believing you won't be harmed by considering "alien" viewpoints is not enough to motivate most people to consider them seriously. You also must be motivated by an *intellectual sense of justice*. You must recognize an *intellectual responsibility* to be fair to views you oppose. You must feel obliged to hear them in their strongest form to ensure that you are not condemning them out of ignorance or bias.

See if you can write out your own description of how the intellectual virtues interrelate. There are many ways to articulate these interrelationships. What is most important is that you clearly understand each virtue, that you see them existing in relationship with one another, and that you consistently and persistently work to cultivate and embody them in your own thinking.

The Spirit of Critical Thinking

Critical thinkers have confidence in their ability to figure out the logic of anything they choose. They continually look for interrelationships and order within systems of ideas. They use the tools of critical thinking every day to improve their thinking, thereby improving their lives.

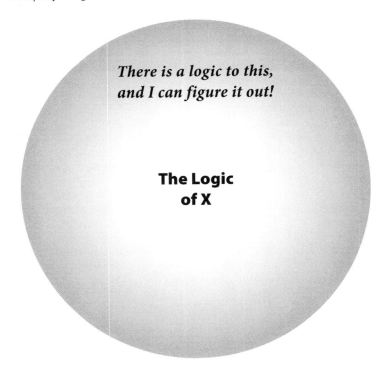

There is a logic to this, and I can figure it out!

**The Logic
of X**

Template for Analyzing the Logic of an Article

Use this template to deconstruct any article, essay, or chapter of a textbook.

The Logic of "(name of the article)"

1) The main purpose of this article is _____.
   (State as accurately as possible the author's purpose for writing the article.)

2) The key question that the author is addressing is _____.
   (Figure out the key question in the mind of the author when s/he wrote the article.)

3) The most important information in this article is _____.
   (Figure out the facts, experiences, and data the author is using to support her/his conclusions.)

4) The main inferences/conclusions in this article are _____.
   (Identify the key conclusions the author comes to and presents in the article.)

5) The key concept(s) we need to understand in this article is (are) _____.
   By these concepts, the author means _____.
   (Figure out the most important ideas you would have to understand in order to understand the author's line of reasoning.)

6) The main assumption(s) underlying the author's thinking is (are) _____.
   (Figure out what the author is taking for granted [that might be questioned].)

7a) If we take this line of reasoning seriously, the implications are _____.
   (What consequences are likely to follow if people take the author's line of reasoning seriously?)

7b) If we fail to take this line of reasoning seriously, the implications are _____.
   (What consequences are likely to follow if people ignore the author's reasoning?)

8) The main point(s) of view presented in this article is (are)_____.
   (What is the author looking at, and how is s/he seeing it?)

Criteria for Evaluating Reasoning

1) **Purpose:** What is the purpose of the reasoner? Is the purpose clearly stated or clearly implied? Is it justifiable?

2) **Question:** Is the question at issue well stated? Is it clear and unbiased? Does the expression of the question do justice to the complexity of the matter at issue? Are the question and purpose directly relevant to each other?

3) **Information:** Does the writer cite relevant evidence, experiences, and/or information essential to the issue? Is the information accurate? Does the writer address the complexities of the issue? Does the writer distort any information or use false information to serve a given interest?

4) **Concepts:** Does the writer clarify key concepts when necessary? Are the concepts used justifiably? Is the writer aware of the concepts that s/he is using in reasoning through the issue?

5) **Assumptions:** Does the writer show a sensitivity to what s/he is taking for granted or assuming (insofar as those assumptions might reasonably be questioned)? Does the writer use questionable assumptions without addressing problems that might be inherent in those assumptions?

6) **Inferences:** Does the writer develop a logical line of reasoning, detailing how s/he arrived at the main conclusions?

7) **Point of View:** Does the writer show sensitivity to alternative relevant points of view or lines of reasoning? Does s/he consider and respond to objections framed from other relevant points of view?

8) **Implications:** Does the writer show a sensitivity to the implications and consequences of the position s/he is taking?

A Template for Problem-Solving

To be an effective problem solver:

1) Figure out, and regularly re-articulate, your goals, purposes, and needs. Recognize problems as obstacles to reaching your goals, achieving your purposes, or satisfying your needs.

2) Wherever possible, take problems one by one. State each problem as clearly and precisely as you can.

3) Study the problem to determine the "kind" of problem you are dealing with. For example, what do you have to do to solve it?

4) Distinguish problems over which you have some control from problems over which you have no control. Concentrate your efforts on problems you can potentially solve.

5) Figure out the information you need to solve the problem. Actively seek that information.

6) Carefully analyze and interpret the information you collect, drawing reasonable inferences.

7) Determine your options for action. What can you do in the short term? In the long term? Recognize your limitations in terms of money, time, and power.

8) Evaluate your options, determining their advantages and disadvantages.

9) Adopt a strategy. Follow through on it. This may involve direct action or a carefully thought-through wait-and-see approach.

10) When you act, monitor the implications of your action. Be ready to revise your strategy if the situation requires it. Be prepared to change your analysis or statement of the problem as more information about the problem becomes available.

Analyzing and Assessing Research

Many research projects are ill defined and focus on a topic rather than an issue or set of issues to be reasoned through. To keep reasoning at the heart of any research you are doing or evaluating, use the following guidelines. They are based in the elements of reasoning and intellectual standards.

1) All research has a fundamental PURPOSE and goal.

- Research purposes and goals should be clearly stated.
- Related purposes should be explicitly distinguished.
- All segments of the research should be relevant to the purpose.
- All research purposes should be realistic and significant.

2) All research addresses a fundamental QUESTION, problem, or issue.

- The fundamental question at issue should be clearly and precisely stated.
- Related questions should be articulated and distinguished.
- All segments of the research should be relevant to the central question.
- All research questions should be realistic and significant.
- All research questions should define clearly stated intellectual tasks that, once fulfilled, will settle the questions.

3) All research identifies data, INFORMATION, and evidence relevant to its fundamental question and purpose.

- All information used should be clear, accurate, and relevant to the fundamental question at issue.
- Information gathered must be sufficient to settle the question at issue.
- Information contrary to the main conclusions of the research should be explained.

4) All research contains INFERENCES or interpretations by which conclusions are drawn.

- All conclusions should be clear, accurate, and relevant to the key question at issue.
- Conclusions drawn should not go beyond what the data imply.
- Conclusions should be consistent and reconcile discrepancies in the data.
- Conclusions should explain how the key questions at issue have been settled.

5) All research is conducted from some POINT OF VIEW or frame of reference.

- All points of view in the research should be identified.
- Objections from competing points of view should be identified and fairly addressed.

6) All research is based on ASSUMPTIONS.

- Clearly identify and assess major assumptions in the research.
- Explain how the assumptions shape the research point of view.

7) All research is expressed through, and shaped by, CONCEPTS and ideas.

- Assess for clarity the key concepts in the research.
- Assess the significance of the key concepts in the research.

8) All research leads somewhere (i.e., has IMPLICATIONS and consequences).

- Trace the implications and consequences that follow from the research.
- Search for negative as well as positive implications.
- Consider all significant implications and consequences.

Three Kinds of Questions

In approaching a question, it is useful to figure out what type it is. Is it a question with one definitive answer? Is it a question that calls for a subjective choice? Or does the question require you to consider competing points of view?

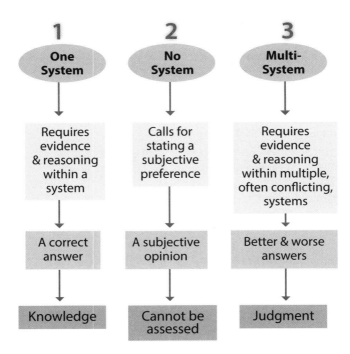

1
One System

⬇

Requires evidence & reasoning within a system

⬇

A correct answer

⬇

Knowledge

2
No System

⬇

Calls for stating a subjective preference

⬇

A subjective opinion

⬇

Cannot be assessed

3
Multi-System

⬇

Requires evidence & reasoning within multiple, often conflicting, systems

⬇

Better & worse answers

⬇

Judgment

There are a number of useful ways to categorize questions for the purpose of analysis. One powerful way is to focus on the type of reasoning required by the question.

Questions of Procedure (established or one system): These include questions with an established procedure or method for finding the answer. These questions are settled by facts, by definition, or both. They are prominent in mathematics, as well as the physical and biological sciences. Examples:

- What is the boiling point of lead?
- What is the size of this room?
- What is the differential of this equation?
- What is the sum of 659 and 979?

Questions of Preference (no system or personal system): Questions with as many answers as there are different human preferences (a category in which subjective taste rules). Examples:

- Which would you prefer: a vacation in the mountains or one at the seashore?
- Do you like to go to the opera? Which is your favorite?
- What color scheme do you prefer in your house?

Questions of Judgment (conflicting systems): Questions requiring reasoning, but with more than one arguable answer. These are questions with better-or-worse answers (well supported and reasoned or poorly supported and/or poorly reasoned). We evaluate answers to these questions using intellectual standards such as clarity, accuracy, relevance, and so on. These questions are predominant in the human disciplines (history, philosophy, economics, sociology, art, etc.). Examples:

- How can we best address the most basic and significant economic problems of the nation today?
- What can be done to significantly reduce the number of people who become addicted to illegal drugs?
- How can we balance business interest and environmental preservation?
- Should capital punishment be abolished?

Three Levels of Thought

We may think of reasoning as occurring at three levels: lower order (entailing very few critical thinking skills), higher order (which is selectively or partially skilled and is only inconsistently fair, if at all), and then highest order (which is both highly skilled and fair). To think at the highest level of quality, we need not only intellectual skills but also intellectual virtues. It is only through cultivating intellectual virtues that reasoning moves to the highest order.

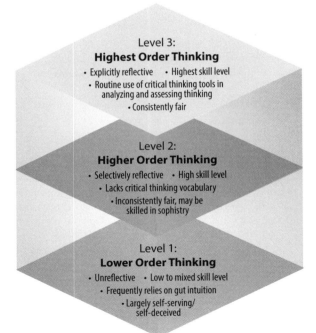

Level 3:
Highest Order Thinking
- Explicitly reflective
- Highest skill level
- Routine use of critical thinking tools in analyzing and assessing thinking
- Consistently fair

Level 2:
Higher Order Thinking
- Selectively reflective
- High skill level
- Lacks critical thinking vocabulary
- Inconsistently fair, may be skilled in sophistry

Level 1:
Lower Order Thinking
- Unreflective
- Low to mixed skill level
- Frequently relies on gut intuition
- Largely self-serving/ self-deceived

The Human Mind Is Frequently Irrational While Having the Capacity for Rational Thought

All humans are innately egocentric and sociocentric. Humans also have (largely undeveloped) rational capacities. Humans begin life as primarily egocentric creatures. Over time, infantile egocentric self-centered thinking merges with sociocentric group-centered thinking. All humans regularly engage in both forms of irrational thought. The extent to which any of us is egocentric or sociocentric is a matter of degree and can change significantly in various situations or contexts. While egocentric and socio-centric propensities are naturally occurring phenomena, rational capacities must be largely developed. It is through the development of rational capacities that we combat irrational tendencies and cultivate critical societies.

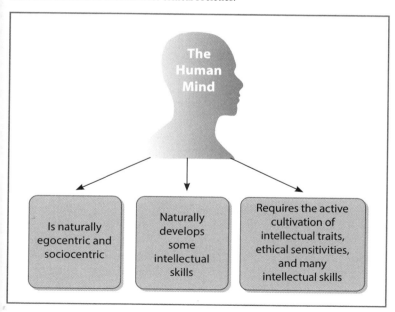

Humans Often Distort Reality Through Irrational Lenses

When engaging in irrational pursuits, the mind must decieve itself; it relies on pathologies of thought to do this. The pathologies of thought can be pictured as a set of filters or lenses that:

- cause or enable us to see the world according to our perceived interests, without regard to others;
- distort reality so we can get what we want; and
- lead us to ignore relevant information to paint a favored picture of the world, based on our vested interests.

These pathologies allow us to decieve ourselves into believing what we want to believe (in order to get what we want or maintain our viewpoint). Pathologies of thought, hence, serve their master—self-deception. They are mainfest in both egocentric and sociocentric thought.

The Problem of Egocentric Thinking

Egocentric thinking results from the unfortunate fact that humans do not naturally consider the rights and needs of others. We do not naturally appreciate the point of view of others or the limitations in our own point of view. We become explicitly aware of our egocentric thinking only if trained to do so. We do not naturally recognize our egocentric assumptions, the egocentric way we use information, the egocentric way we interpret data, the source of our egocentric concepts and ideas, or the implications of our egocentric thought. We do not naturally recognize our self-serving perspective.

As humans we live with the unrealistic but confident sense that we have fundamentally figured out the way things actually are, and that we have done this objectively. We naturally believe in our intuitive perceptions, however inaccurate they may be. Instead of using intellectual standards in thinking, we often use self-centered psychological standards to determine what to believe and what to reject. Here are the most commonly used psychological standards in human thinking.

"IT'S TRUE BECAUSE I BELIEVE IT." Innate egocentrism: I assume that what I believe is true even though I have never questioned the basis for many of my beliefs.

"IT'S TRUE BECAUSE WE BELIEVE IT." Innate sociocentrism: I assume that the dominant beliefs of the groups to which I belong are true even though I have never questioned the basis for those beliefs.

"IT'S TRUE BECAUSE I WANT TO BELIEVE IT." Innate wish fulfillment: I believe in whatever puts me (or the groups to which I belong) in a positive light. I believe what "feels good," what does not require me to change my thinking in any significant way and/or what does not require me to admit I have been wrong.

"IT'S TRUE BECAUSE I HAVE ALWAYS BELIEVED IT." Innate self-validation: I have a strong desire to maintain beliefs that I have long held, even though I have not seriously considered the extent to which those beliefs are justified by the evidence.

"IT'S TRUE BECAUSE IT IS IN MY BEST INTEREST TO BELIEVE IT." Innate selfishness: I believe whatever justifies my getting more power, money, or personal advantage even though these beliefs are not grounded in sound reasoning or evidence.

Feelings That Accompany Egocentrism

These are some of the many feelings that might accompany egocentric thinking. They often occur when egocentric thinking is "unsuccessful." Note that some of these emotions may be concomitant with rational thought—depending on the context and particulars in a given case.

When egocentric thinking is successful in getting what it wants, positive feelings accompany it. But when egocentric thinking is not able to achieve its purposes, negative feelings result.

The Problem of Sociocentric Thinking

Most people do not understand the degree to which they have uncritically internalized the dominant prejudices of their society or culture. Sociologists and anthropologists identify this condition as the state of being "culture bound." This phenomenon is caused by sociocentric thinking, which includes:

- The uncritical tendency to place one's culture, nation, and/or religion above all others.
- The uncritical tendency to select self-serving positive descriptions of ourselves and negative descriptions of those who think differently from us.
- The uncritical tendency to internalize group norms and beliefs, take on group identities, and act as we are expected to act—without the least sense that what we are doing might reasonably be questioned.
- The tendency to blindly conform to group restrictions (many of which are arbitrary or coercive).
- The failure to think beyond the traditional prejudices of one's culture.
- The failure to study and internalize the insights of other cultures (improving thereby the breadth and depth of one's thinking).
- The failure to distinguish universal ethics from relativistic cultural requirements and taboos.
- The failure to realize that mass media in every culture shapes the news from the point of view of that culture.
- The failure to think historically and anthropologically (and hence to be trapped in current ways of thinking).
- The failure to see sociocentric thinking as a significant impediment to intellectual development.

Sociocentric thinking is a hallmark of an uncritical society. It can be diminished only when replaced by cross-cultural, fairminded thinking—critical thinking in the strong sense.

Primary Forms of Sociocentric Thought

Consider four distinct forms of sociocentric thought. These forms function and are manifest in complex relationships with one another; all are destructive.[1] They can be summarized as follows:

1. *Groupishness[2] (or group selfishness)*—the tendency on the part of groups to seek the most for the in-group without regard to the rights and needs of others, in order to advance the group's biased interests. Groupishness is almost certainly the primary tendency in sociocentric thinking, the foundational driving force behind it (probably connected to survival in our dim dark past). Everyone in the group is privileged; everyone outside the group is denied group privileges and/or seen as a potential threat.

2. *Group validation*—the tendency on the part of groups to believe their way is the right way and their views are the correct views; the tendency to reinforce one another in these beliefs; the inclination to validate the group's views, however dysfunctional or illogical. These may be long-held or newly established views, but in either case, they are perceived by the group to be true and, in many cases, to advance its interests. This tendency informs the worldview from which everyone outside the group is seen and understood and by which everything that happens outside the group is judged. It leads to the problem of in-group thinking and behavior—everyone inside the group thinks within a collective logic; everyone outside the group is judged according to the standards and beliefs of the in-group.

---

[1] The term "sociocentric thought" is reserved for those group beliefs that cause harm or are likely to cause harm. Group thought that is reasonable, useful, or helpful would not fall into this category.

[2] By groupishness, we mean group selfishness. This term refers to group pursuit of its interests without sufficient regard for the rights and needs of those outside the group. Its counterpart is selfishness, which refers to individual pursuit of one's interests without sufficient regard for the rights and needs of others.

3. *Group control*—the tendency on the part of groups to ensure that group members behave in accordance with group expectations. This logic guides the intricate inner workings of the group, largely through enforcement, ostracism, and punishment in connection with group customs, conventions, rules, taboos, mores, and laws. Group control can also take the form of "recruitment" through propaganda and other forms of manipulation. It is often sophisticated and camouflaged.

4. *Group conformity*—a byproduct of the fact that in order to survive, people must figure out how to fit themselves into the groups they are thrust into or voluntarily choose to join. They must conform to the rules and laws set down by those in control. Dissenters are punished in numerous ways. Group control and group conformity are two sides of the same coin—each presupposes the other.

These four sociocentric tendencies interrelate and overlap in any number of ways and thus should be understood as four parts of an interconnected puzzle.

Sociocentric tendencies largely lie at the unconscious level. It isn't that people are aware of these tendencies and consciously choose to go along with them. Rather, these dispositions are, at least to some extent, hidden by self-deception, rationalization, and other native mechanisms of the mind that keep us from seeing and facing the truth in our thoughts and actions. The mind tells itself one thing on the surface (e.g., we are being fair to all involved) when in fact it is acting upon a different thought entirely (e.g., we are mainly concerned with our own interests). In most instances, the mind can find ways to justify itself—even when engaging in highly unethical acts.

It should be pointed out that there are many circumstances in which rational behavior might be confused with sociocentric behavior. For instance, group members may well validate among themselves views that are reasonable. Groups should also expect group members to behave in ethical ways.

Unethical Pursuit of Group Agendas

Focused on getting the most for a group, Groupishness (or Group Selfishness) is driven by these sociocentric forces:

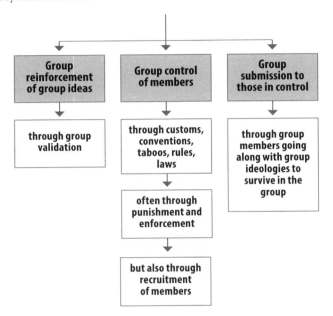

Groupishness, to be effectively achieved, requires group reinforcement, group control, and group submission. This diagram begins to illuminate the complex relationships among the four primary forms of sociocentric thought.

Envisioning Critical Societies

The critical habit of thought, if usual in society, will pervade all its mores, because it is a way of taking up the problems of life. Men educated in it cannot be stampeded by stump orators. . . . They are slow to believe. They can hold things as possible or probable in all degrees, without certainty and without pain. They can wait for evidence and weigh evidence, uninfluenced by the emphasis or confidence with which assertions are made on one side or the other. They can resist appeals to their dearest prejudices and all kinds of cajolery. Education in the critical faculty is the only education of which it can be truly said that it makes good citizens.

William Graham Sumner, 1906

Humans have the capacity to be rational and fair, but this capacity must be cultivated. It will be significantly developed only if critical societies emerge. Critical societies will develop only to the extent that:

- Critical thinking is viewed as essential to living a reasonable and fairminded life.
- Critical thinking is routinely taught and consistently fostered.
- The problematics of thinking are an abiding concern.
- Closed-mindedness is systemically discouraged; open-mindedness is systematically encouraged.
- Intellectual integrity, intellectual humility, intellectual empathy, confidence in reason, and intellectual courage are social values.
- Egocentric and sociocentric thinking are recognized as a bane in social life.
- Children are routinely taught that the rights and needs of others are equal to their own.
- A multicultural worldview is fostered.
- People are encouraged to think for themselves and discouraged from uncritically accepting the thinking or behavior of others.
- People routinely study and diminish irrational thought.
- People internalize universal intellectual standards.

If we want critical societies, we must create them.

20 BARRIERS TO CRITICAL SOCIETIES

To illustrate the fact that we as humans tend not to take thinking seriously in today's cultures, consider the following 20 barriers to critical societies. Most people:

1. are only superficially aware of critical thinking.

2. cannot clearly articulate the ideal of critical thinking, know of it only as a positive buzz term, and, in any case, habitually violate its standards in multiple ways. Most humans, in other words, have not aspired to the ideal of critical thought, and most who have done so (having only an implicit idea of it) have succeeded only modestly.

3. uncritically accept the traditional, mainstream views and beliefs of their culture.

4. are "culture bound" (enslaved within social conventions).

5. uncritically accept the views of authority figures.

6. are not aware of, and do not attempt to explicitly use, intellectual standards in their thinking.

7. do not understand human thinking (their own or others') or the impediments to reasonability.

8. (unconsciously) believe much that is arbitrary or irrational.

9. uncritically accept bureaucratic rules, procedures, and formulas.

10. accept a variety of forms of authoritarianism (such as blindly following a religious ideology).

11. are uncreative and unoriginal.

12. are trapped in their social class.

13. never come to think well within any subject and have no sense of what it is to think beyond subject-matter compartments.

14. do not believe in freedom of thought and speech or in a wide range of other inalienable freedoms.

15. are biased on questions of gender, culture, species, and politics.

16. use their intellects only superficially.

17. have little command over their primitive emotions and desires; rather, they tend to be at the mercy of their own irrational impulses and passions.

18. do not value true spontaneity, naturalness, or artlessness.

19. are unable and/or unwilling to think within the viewpoints of others who hold a different worldview.

20. are unable to achieve self-actualization, self-command, or enlightenment because they lack command of their thoughts, as well as understanding of the relationship between thoughts and emotions.

It Is Essential to Distinguish Among Questions of Ethics, Social Conventions, Religion, and the Law

If we hope for fairminded critical societies in the long run, the majority of humans will need to distinguish between ethics and other, distinctly different, modes of thinking that are currently confused with ethics across human societies. Though overlap exists between these diverse modes of thought, it is essential to understand the ways in which they are markedly dissimilar. Most important, ethical reasoning must be disconnected from other modes of thought so that one can then turn to, and internalize, principles most proper for use in reasoning through ethical questions or problems.

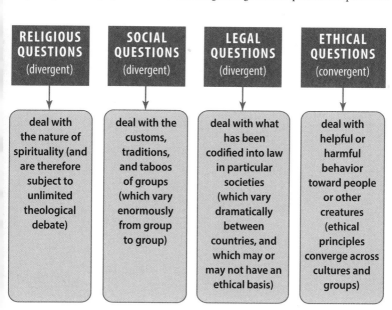

RELIGIOUS QUESTIONS (divergent)

deal with the nature of spirituality (and are therefore subject to unlimited theological debate)

SOCIAL QUESTIONS (divergent)

deal with the customs, traditions, and taboos of groups (which vary enormously from group to group)

LEGAL QUESTIONS (divergent)

deal with what has been codified into law in particular societies (which vary dramatically between countries, and which may or may not have an ethical basis)

ETHICAL QUESTIONS (convergent)

deal with helpful or harmful behavior toward people or other creatures (ethical principles converge across cultures and groups)

Any given religious, social, or legal edict or practice may, or may not, be ethical in orientation. If we are ever to reach a point in human development where skilled ethical reasoning is the norm, each of us must cultivate in ourselves the ability to determine whether any belief system, practice, rule, or law is ethical. Being skilled in ethical reasoning means developing a conscience not subservient to fluctuating social conventions, theological systems, or unethical laws.

As we face problems in our lives, we must distinguish the ethical from the unethical (or the pseudo-ethical), and we must routinely apply ethical principles to those problems that are genuinely ethical in nature. The more often we do so, the better we become at ethical reasoning.